Natalie Dormady

365

GENTLE REMINDERS

LIMINAL 11

TO MY
MOM AND DAD
THANK YOU AND
I LOVE YOU.

LIMINAL 11

This edition published in 2020 by Liminal 11

First published in 2019 by Liminal 11

Copyright © 2019, 2020 Natalie Dormady

Written and illustrated by Natalie Dormady
This edition published in 2020 by Liminal 11

Book design by Sara Botero

Cover design by Mike Medaglia

Printed in China

ISBN 978-1-912634-27-9

10 9 8 7 6 5 4 3 2 1

www.liminal11.com

INTRODUCTION

Doodling rainbows reminds me that storms always end and the light will return. Drawing flowers and bumblebees reminds me of how important we each are in this world.

The book you are holding began while I was struggling with an eating disorder and my mental health. There was a moment in one of my support sessions when I was asked to show how my life looked both with and without the eating disorder. I chose to communicate this through illustration. To be able to safely express my thoughts and feelings visually was the first step in a journey that lead me here.

For their support along the way I would sincerely like to thank Nic, Jen, Kim, Kathryn, Gram, and all my family. A big thank you to my editor Mike and all my friends at Liminal 11.

But most of all, thank you April and Lynette.

My hope is that this book may bring you comfort, light and joy. And remember – you are enough – it's okay to take your time – self-care is not selfish – and, most importantly, you are not alone.

From your friend,

Natalie Dormady

IT'S OK
TO TAKE
YOUR

January 1

YOUR FEELINGS   ARE VALID.

January 2

January 3

January 4

YOU ARE NOT
YOUR PAST

January 5

January 6

January 7

January 8

January 9

January 10

January 11

ONE DAY
AT A TIME
ONE STEP
AT A TIME
ONE BREATH
AT A TIME

January 12

YOU WERE ENOUGH YESTERDAY.

YOU ARE ENOUGH TODAY.

YOU WILL ALWAYS BE ENOUGH.

January 13

GOING SLOWLY
IS OKAY TOO.

January 14

January 15

YOU ARE ALLOWED
TO FEEL YOUR
EMOTIONS.
EACH
&
EVERY
ONE.

January 16

YOU ARE
HERE
+
YOU ARE
ENOUGH

January 17

January 18

YOU ARE
CAPABLE
OF MORE THAN
YOU THINK.

January 19

January 20

BELIEVE IN YOURSELF

... OK?

January 21

January 22

IT IS OKAY TO REST

January 23

I AM ENOUGH & I AM TRYING MY VERY BEST.

January 24

SAYING NO
IS PERFECTLY
OKAY

January 25

ONE DAY AT A TIME

January 26

TAKE
CARE OF
YOURSELF

January 27

YOUR ANXIETY
IS NOT YOUR FAULT

January 28

January 29

January 30

January 31

it's okay to be PROUD of how far you've come.

February 1

February 2

IT'S OKAY TO
TAKE A BREAK.

February 3

IT'S
OKAY
TO BE
STRUGGLING

It's ALSO OKAY TO
ASK FOR HELP

February 4

YOU DESERVE TO
GET BETTER

February 5

February 6

February 7

February 8

IT'S OK TO
LET GO

February 9

February 10

YOU DESERVE
TO GET BETTER.

February 11

HAVE
PATIENCE
WITH
YOURSELF
TOO.

February 12

YOUR
MENTAL HEALTH
IS A PRIORITY.

February 13

February 14

YOU ARE
LOVED
SO MUCH
MORE THAN
YOU KNOW.

February 15

BE GENTLE WITH
YOURSELF
TOO.

February 16

GIVE YOURSELF TIME TO HEAL

February 17

SENDING LOVE

SENDING LIGHT

YOU WILL GET
THROUGH THIS
AND
YOU WILL BE
ALRIGHT.

February 18

February 19

SELF CARE
iS NOT
SELFiSH

February 20

February 21

TAKE CARE OF YOURSELF

February 22

YOUR BEST
MAY LOOK DIFFERENT
FROM DAY TO DAY

AND THAT
IS OKAY.

February 23

PLACE
YOUR HAND
ON YOUR
HEART
AND TAKE
A DEEP
BREATH.
YOU ARE
ENOUGH
AND YOU ARE
TRYING YOUR
B E S T

February 24

February 25

February 26

February 27

FEELING AND HEALING

February 28

March 1

YOU ARE LOVED

March 2

March 3

ONE DAY
AT A TIME

March 4

YOU
MATTER

March 5

sending light.

YOU ARE NOT
ALONE IN THIS

March 6

IT IS OKAY
TO ACCEPT
SUPPORT.

IT IS OKAY
TO ASK FOR SUPPORT.

March 7

March 8

March 9

March 10

APPRECIATE
YOURSELF
TOO

March 11

YOU
ARE SO
IMPORTANT
AND
YOUR LIFE
MATTERS.

March 12

March 13

March 14

IT IS OKAY
TO REST

March 15

SOME DAYS FEEL
LiKE
MOUNTAINS

SOME FEEL LiKE SMALL HiLLS

AND SiDEWALK
TRAILS

YOU CAN MAKE iT
THROUGH THIS.

March 16

March 17

IT'S OKAY
TO GO

AT YOUR
OWN PACE

March 18

March 19

IT IS OKAY
TO BE PROUD OF
YOURSELF

March 20

YOU ARE

ALLOWED

TO CHANGE

March 21

March 22

YOU ARE MORE THAN A NUMBER.

March 23

BEE
PATIENT
WITH
YOURSELF

March 24

March 25

SELF - CARE
iS NOT
SELFiSH.

March 26

March 27

YOU ARE STRONGER THAN YOU THINK.

March 28

March 29

March 30

YOU ARE
ENOUGH

March 31

YOU ARE
NOT ALONE.

April 1

April 2

YOU DESERVE TO
BEE HAPPY.

April 3

BE GENTLE
WITH YOURSELF
TOO.

April 4

YOU ARE
STRONGER
THAN YOU
THINK.

April 5

April 6

April 7

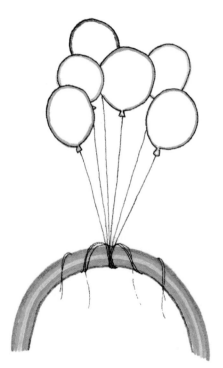

IT'S OK
TO ASK
FOR HELP.

April 8

April 9

IT'S OK TO BE
PROUD OF YOURSELF

April 10

THE WAVES WILL PASS

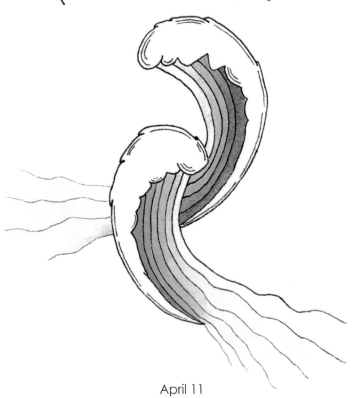

April 11

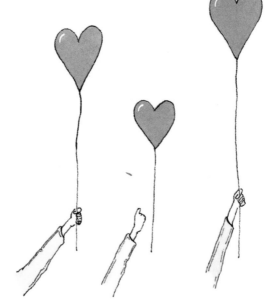

April 12

April 13

April 14

TAKING MY TIME

AND THAT
IS OKAY

April 15

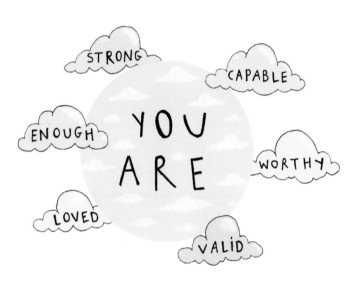

STRONG
CAPABLE
ENOUGH
YOU ARE
WORTHY
LOVED
VALID

April 16

April 17

CELEBRATE
EVERY TINY
VICTORY

April 18

IT'S OK TO
ASK FOR HELP

April 19

YOUR RECOVERY is VALID

April 20

April 21

BE PATIENT WITH YOURSELF TOO. HEALING TAKES TIME.

April 22

April 23

you are....

CAPABLE

BRAVE

ENOUGH

WORTHY

April 24

YOU ARE
SO VERY
IMPORTANT.

April 25

IT IS OKAY TO TAKE YOUR TIME

April 26

IT IS
OKAY
TO BE
PROUD OF
YOURSELF

April 27

YOU ARE
ALLOWED
TO CHANGE

April 28

THESE CLOUDS WILL PASS

April 29

April 30

YOU MATTER

May 1

May 2

May 3

May 4

May 5

May 6

YOU ARE
ALLOWED
TO TAKE UP
SPACE.

May 7

RECOVERY TAKES TIME

May 8

THESE WAVES WILL PASS

May 9

YOUR FEELINGS
ARE IMPORTANT

YOUR FEELINGS
ARE VALID

YOUR FEELINGS
MATTER

May 10

May 11

IT'S OK TO ASK
FOR SUPPORT

May 12

YOU
HAVE A
PURPOSE.

May 13

BE
PATIENT
WITH
YOURSELF
TOO.

May 14

May 15

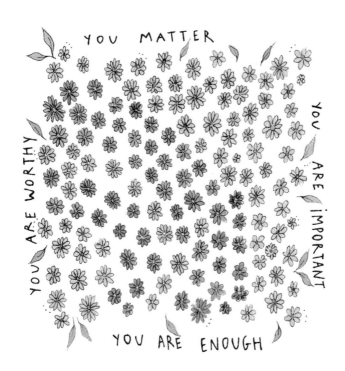

May 16

May 17

IT'S OKAY
TO TAKE ONE
STEP AT A TIME.

May 18

DON'T
FORGET
HOW FAR
YOU'VE
COME

May 19

YOU CAN & WILL MAKE IT THROUGH THIS

May 20

SMALL
PROGRESS
IS STILL PROGRESS

May 21

BE GENTLE
WITH YOURSELF
AS WELL.

May 22

I HOPE YOU KNOW
THAT YOU MATTER
SO VERY MUCH.

May 23

May 24

YOU'RE CAPABLE OF
MORE THAN YOU THINK.

May 25

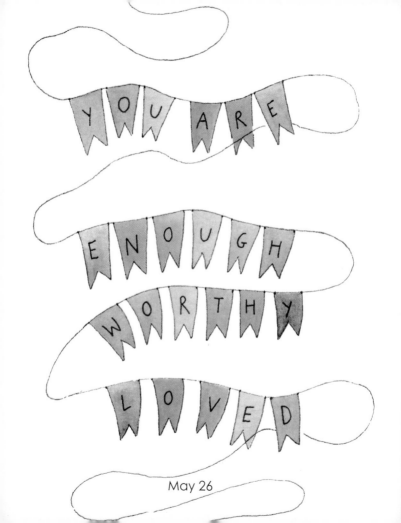

May 26

IT iS
OKAY
TO CHANGE

May 27

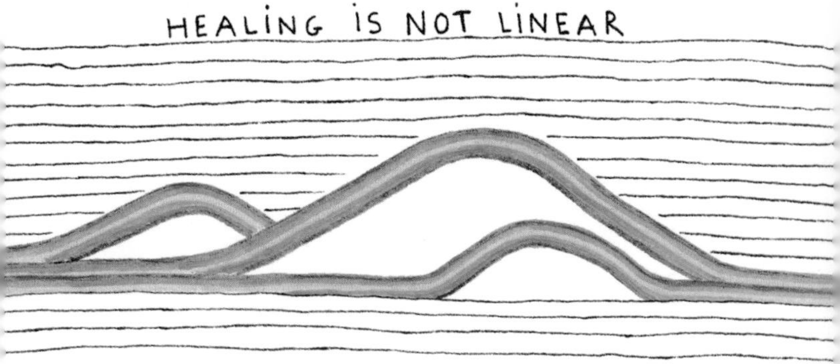

HEALING IS NOT LINEAR

May 28

May 29

YOU ARE CAPABLE
YOU ARE ENOUGH
YOU ARE BRAVE

May 30

YOU ARE
SUCH AN
IMPORTANT
PART OF THIS WORLD.

May 31

BE GENTLE
WITH YOURSELF

June 1

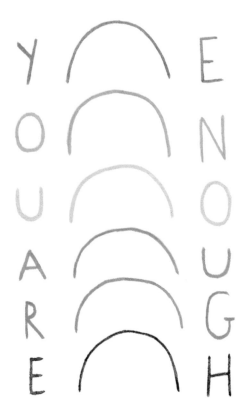

Y O U A R E

E N O U G H

June 2

THESE WAVES WILL PASS

June 3

YOU
DESERVE
TO HEAL

June 4

SELF CARE IS NOT SELFISH

June 5

June 6

June 7

YOU ARE
AN IMPORTANT
PART OF THIS
WORLD

June 8

I AM ENOUGH

June 9

IT'S OK TO HEAL
AT YOUR OWN PACE

June 10

YOUR
MENTAL HEALTH
MATTERS
TOO

June 11

YOU ARE
SO MUCH MORE
THAN YOUR
DISORDER

June 12

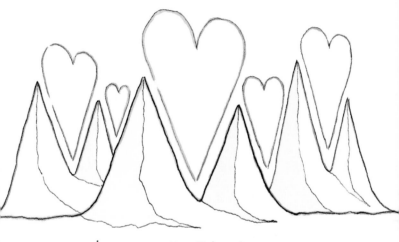

IT IS OKAY TO ASK FOR
SUPPORT.
. YOU ARE NOT ALONE
IN THIS.

June 13

YOU
DESERVE
TO FEEL
FREE

June 14

SLOW PROGRESS is STILL PROGRESS

June 15

THIS WiLL PASS

June 16

June 17

REST.

IT IS OK.

June 18

IT IS
OKAY
TO TAKE
YOUR TIME

June 19

IT'S OK TO GO
AND TO GROW
AT YOUR OWN PACE

June 20

YOU DESERVE

TO BE HAPPY

June 21

EVERYTHING
YOU FEEL
IS OKAY

June 22

YOUR FEELINGS
MATTER

YOUR THOUGHTS
MATTER

YOU MATTER

June 23

June 24

YOU ARE
SUCH AN
IMPORTANT
PART OF THIS
W O R L D .

June 25

BELIEVE
IN
YOURSELF
TOO.

June 26

June 27

June 28

YOU DESERVE TO
BE HAPPY.

June 29

June 30

IT'S OK
TO TAKE
YOUR TIME
HEALING
AND
FEELING.

July 1

July 2

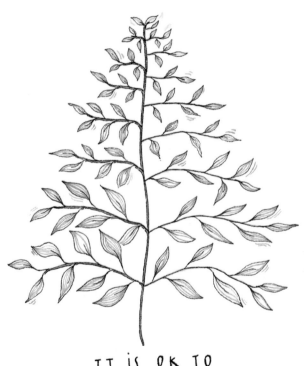

IT IS OK TO
F E E L

July 3

WORD SEARCH

W O R T H Y K Z i
C J M R B P Q G M
Z L Q Y X W E M P
T D E V O L N Q O
H P S X B Y O i R
F E F A S P U X T
B Q P D L N G Z A
G A Z N V S H S N
C D i L A V Q A T

i AM

·IMPORTANT·
·LOVED ·WORTHY · VALID
·ENOUGH ·CAPABLE ·SAFE

July 4

July 5

YOU ARE
IMPORTANT
AND YOU MATTER

July 6

IT IS OKAY
TO ASK FOR
SUPPORT.

July 7

ALLOW

YOUR
THOUGHTS
&
FEELINGS
TO TRAVEL
&
PASS

July 8

YOU'RE
STRONGER
THAN YOU
KNOW

July 9

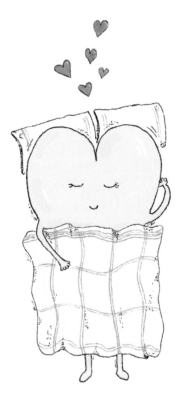

IT IS OKAY
TO REST.

YOU ARE
DOING
YOUR
BEST.

July 10

YOU ARE CAPABLE
OF SO MUCH MORE
THAN YOU THINK

July 11

YOU ARE
WORTHY
ENOUGH
IMPORTANT
LOVED

July 12

July 13

July 14

July 15

YOU ARE
STRONGER
THAN YOU THINK

July 16

THIS
IS ONLY
TEMPORARY

July 17

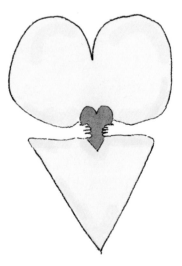

BE KiND TO
YOURSELF
AS WELL

July 18

YOU DESERVE TO BELiEVE iN

YOURSELF

July 19

YOU DESERVE TO

HEAL

July 20

July 21

NEVER
APOLOGIZE
FOR BEING
WHO YOU
ARE.

July 22

July 23

YOU BELONG HERE

July 24

IT'S
OKAY
TO REST.

July 25

ONE DAY AT A TIME.

July 26

July 27

YOU ARE
ENOUGH.

July 28

July 29

iT iS
OKAY
TO CHANGE
YOUR
MiND.

July 30

GIVE
YOURSELF
TIME

July 31

YOU ARE CAPABLE OF
EXTRAORDINARY
THINGS

August 1

HEALING
TAKES
TIME

August 2

August 3

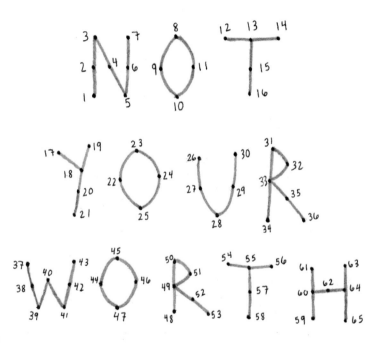

August 4

August 5

YOU ARE LOVED
AND YOU MATTER
SO MUCH

August 6

IT'S OK TO GO SLOWLY.

August 7

August 8

YOUR FEELINGS
ARE VALID.

August 9

IT'S
OKAY
TO TAKE
A BREAK.

August 10

August 11

YOU ARE ENOUGH

August 12

YOU ARE
IMPORTANT
AND YOU
MATTER

August 13

YOU ARE
ALLOWED
TO CHANGE

August 14

YOU ARE SO VERY IMPORTANT

August 15

August 16

IT'S OKAY
TO BE PROUD
OF YOURSELF

August 17

IT IS OKAY
TO GO
SLOWLY

August 18

it is ok to rest.

August 19

YOU ARE CAPABLE

August 20

August 21

YOUR FEELINGS MATTER

August 22

HEALING TAKES TIME

August 23

YOU ARE LOVED
MORE THAN YOU
KNOW.

August 24

HAVE PATIENCE
WITH YOURSELF TOO.

August 25

August 26

August 27

IT IS OKAY TO
ACCEPT SUPPORT

August 28

THIS is
TEMPORARY.

August 29

August 30

August 31

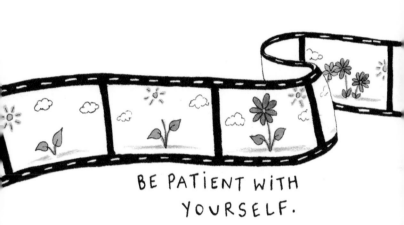

BE PATIENT WITH
YOURSELF.

September 1

i
AM
ENOUGH

September 2

YOU ARE NOT ALONE iN THiS

September 3

September 4

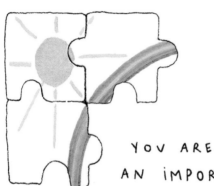

YOU ARE
AN IMPORTANT
PART OF THIS
WORLD.

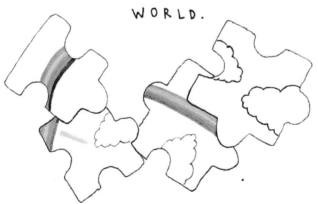

September 5

YOU ARE
CAPABLE
OF MORE THAN
YOU THINK.

September 6

IT'S OKAY TO TAKE A BREAK

September 7

September 8

YOU ARE
LOVED
MORE
THAN YOU
KNOW

September 9

SELF-CARE
iS NOT
SELFiSH

September 10

YOU ARE STRONGER THAN YOU THINK

September 11

YOU ARE ENOUGH

September 12

IT'S OK TO GO
AND TO GROW
AT YOUR OWN PACE.

September 13

September 14

YOU ARE IMPORTANT

September 15

IT'S OK
TO DO
WHAT IS
BEST FOR
YOU.

September 16

YOU ARE

LOVED

September 17

IT iS OKAY TO
TAKE A BREAK

September 18

YOUR FEELINGS
MATTER
YOUR FEELINGS
ARE VALID

September 19

BE GENTLE
WITH YOURSELF

September 20

IT IS OK
TO FEEL.
TO HEAL.

September 21

September 22

IT'S OKAY TO
F E E L
P R O U D
OF YOURSELF

September 23

STORMS WILL PASS
AND THE SUN WILL
COME BACK.

September 24

YOU ARE
MORE THAN
YOUR ILLNESS.

September 25

September 26

September 27

IT IS OKAY
TO REST

September 28

YOUR
MENTAL
HEALTH
MATTERS

September 29

YOUR FEELINGS
ARE VALID.

September 30

NEVER APOLOGIZE
FOR BEING WHO
YOU ARE.

October 1

YOU ARE CAPABLE

October 2

October 3

October 4

YOU
ARE
LOVED
WORTHY
IMPORTANT

October 5

October 6

FRYING
TRYING

October 7

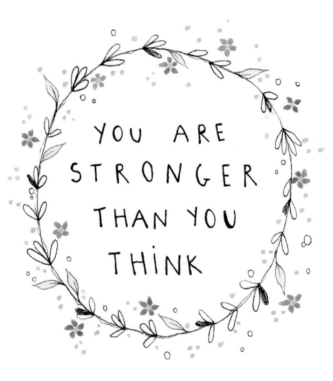

YOU ARE STRONGER THAN YOU THINK

October 8

IT'S OK
TO GO &
TO GROW
AT YOUR
OWN PACE

October 9

October 10

YOU ARE
NOT YOUR
iLLNESS

October 11

IT IS OKAY TO
REACH OUT

October 12

YOU ARE
CAPABLE
OF MORE
THAN YOU
THINK.

October 13

October 14

October 15

YOU ARE WORTHY OF BELONGING

October 16

SLOW DAYS
ARE IMPORTANT
DAYS TOO.

October 17

October 18

October 19

October 20

YOU ARE
ALLOWED
to CHANGE.

October 21

YOU
DESERVE
TO
HEAL.

October 22

WE
BELIEVE
IN
YOU

October 23

ONE DAY AT A TIME.

October 24

YOU ARE NOT ALONE
IN THIS.

October 25

THIS WILL PASS

October 26

October 27

YOU ARE IMPORTANT

October 28

October 29

October 30

IT'S OK
TO NOT
BE OK.

October 31

HEALING TAKES TIME

November 1

YOU ARE ALLOWED TO CHANGE

November 2

BE PATIENT WITH
YOURSELF
TOO.

November 3

YOU ARE
IMPORTANT
AND
YOU MATTER

November 4

IT IS
OKAY
TO ASK
FOR SUPPORT

November 5

November 6

it's ok
to make
mistakes.

November 7

YOU ARE
STRONGER
THAN YOU THINK
YOU ARE
CAPABLE
OF MORE THAN YOU KNOW

November 8

November 9

November 10

BEE
GENTLE
WITH
YOURSELF

November 11

YOU ARE
NOT ALONE
IN THIS.

November 12

November 13

November 14

DON'T GIVE UP, OK?

November 15

YOU ARE LOVED.
YOU ARE IMPORTANT.

November 16

YOU DESERVE
TO BE HAPPY

November 17

IT'S OK
TO DO WHAT'S
BEST FOR YOU.

November 18

YOU DON'T NEED
SOCIAL APPROVAL

November 19

IT'S OK
TO LET
GO.

November 20

YOU ARE ENOUGH

November 21

November 22

November 23

IT IS OKAY TO PUT
YOURSELF
AND YOUR
NEEDS
FIRST

November 24

November 25

GIVE YOURSELF
TIME.

November 26

NEVER APOLOGIZE
FOR BEING
WHO YOU
ARE.

November 27

YOU ARE LOVED.

November 28

GIVE YOURSELF TIME.
TO GROW.
TO HEAL.

November 29

November 30

It is OKAY TO TAKE MY TIME

December 1

December 2

YOU ARE LOVED
SO MUCH MORE
THAN YOU
KNOW

December 3

APPRECIATE YOURSELF AS WELL

December 4

YOU HAVE A PURPOSE

December 5

December 6

YOU
DESERVE
TO
HEAL

December 7

THESE
CLOUDS
WILL
PASS

December 8

December 9

December 10

December 11

December 12

IT iS
OKAY
TO TAKE
YOUR TIME

December 13

A WHALEY GENTLE REMINDER

B R E A T H E

December 14

ONE DAY
AT A TIME.

December 15

December 16

YOU ARE
STRONGER
THAN YOU
THINK.

December 17

December 18

BE GENTLE WITH
YOURSELF
AS WELL

December 19

December 20

YOU DESERVE
TO HEAL

December 21

December 22

December 23

BE GENTLE WITH
YOURSELF TOO.

December 24

December 25

December 26

December 27

YOU ARE ENOUGH AND YOU ALWAYS WILL BE

December 28

HAVE PATIENCE WITH
YOURSELF
AS WELL

December 29

YOU ARE STRONGER THAN YOU THINK.

December 30

KEEP ON GOING.
KEEP ON GROWING.

December 31